BODY ARTS
THE HISTORY OF TATTOOING AND BODY MODIFICATION™

TATTOO REMOVAL

Nicholas Faulkner and Frank Spalding

Rosen
YA
New York

Published in 2019 by The Rosen Publishing Group, Inc.
29 East 21st Street, New York, NY 10010

First Edition

Cataloging-in-Publication Data

Names: Faulkner, Nicholas, author. | Spalding, Frank, author.
Title: Tattoo removal / Nicholas Faulkner and Frank Spalding.
Description: New York : Rosen Publishing, 2019. | Series: Body arts : the history of tattooing and body modification | Includes bibliographical references and index. | Audience: Grades 9–12.
Identifiers: ISBN 9781508180791 (library bound) | ISBN 9781508180807 (pbk.)
Subjects: LCSH: Tattoo removal. | Skin—Laser surgery. | Tattooing.
Classification: LCC RL120.L37 F38 2019 | DDC 617.4'770598—dc23

Manufactured in the United States of America

CONTENTS

INTRODUCTION

Tattoos are more popular than ever these days. And with this growing popularity comes an increase in tattoo removal. As of 2016, 36 percent of adults 18 to 25 have at least one tattoo. Seventeen percent of people who get tattoos later on have regrets. And about 1 in 10 people with tattoos are planning to have or have had one removed.

Though tattoos are meant to be lifelong commitments, people often get them as the result of snap decisions. Even if the tattoo was well thought-out, people's tastes and values change over time in ways they can never predict. Since tattoos have gone mainstream, many people get them without giving too much thought as to how much they will like their tattoos several years down the road.

But just as getting the tattoo is a major commitment, so is getting it removed. It is often a long, uncomfortable, and expensive process. You have to do your research. There's a variety of removal methods and you'll need to speak to your dermatologist about the one that's best for you.

Tattoo removal is expensive—often much too expensive for young people to be able to afford. To help

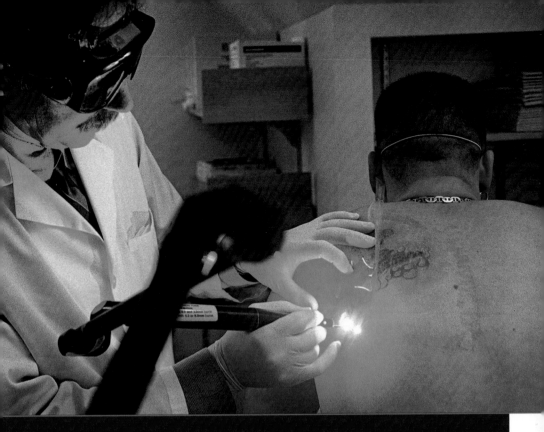

There are a number of methods of tattoo removal. Laser treatment is among the most popular and least invasive techniques.

offset the costs, some organizations have created programs to pay for the removal of tattoos, mainly gang tattoos. Sometimes, the cost of removing the tattoo is provided outright; other times, applicants for this program are required to undergo counseling or perform community service in return for the removal treatments or a discount on tattoo removal fees. These programs generally favor laser tattoo removal.

For former gang members, tattoo removal can be serious business. Many of them get gang-related tattoos—often done by amateurs—when they are in their teens. Sometimes, this is part of the gang initiation. For those who want to move on and put their time as a gang member behind them, these tattoos can be a major obstacle to establishing their future lives.

Laser removal is by far the most popular removal method. Though it can be painful, it's the least invasive, meaning it doesn't puncture the skin. And it generally produces the best results. People have likened the sensation to repeated bee stings. But there are other options, too, such as intense pulse light therapy, surgical excision, and dermabrasion. You can also have the tattoo covered up with another tattoo.

The easiest way to avoid having one removed, though, is to not get one in the first place that you'll grow to regret. Tattoo removal should be part of the decision to get a tattoo from the start. Even though you can get the ink removed from your skin, it's never fully gone. There are always slight remnants and scarring that can't be erased. So in this way, a tattoo is truly permanent.

Carefully consider how much you want that piece of body art and how you and others will view it in the future. Does it mean something more to you than mere decoration? If not, then you might not value it in a few years as your tastes change. If you're committed to getting the tattoo, hang the design up on your wall for several weeks to see if you grow bored of it. It's better to remove it from your wall than your body. Then, do careful research on your tattoo artist. Many people regret their tattoos not because of the design they choose, but because the tattoo was simply of inferior quality. There are artists of all types, from the highly professional to those who shouldn't be in the profession.

If you do have a tattoo or tattoos that you want removed, know that you have options. But do your research. Talk to multiple professionals, such as a dermatologist and your physician. You want to be sure that you're not only getting the proper treatment, but also that it's safe and will produce the desired results.

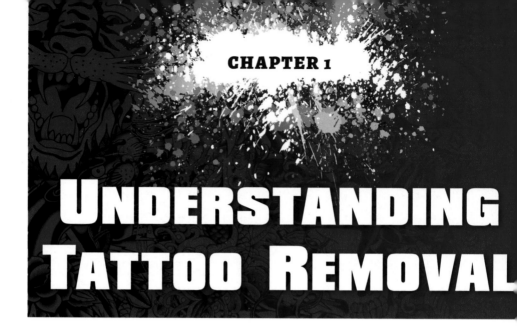

CHAPTER 1

UNDERSTANDING TATTOO REMOVAL

Before getting a tattoo removed—or before getting a tattoo at all—you should understand what's involved in the removal process. There's no getting around it; tattoo removal is often a long and difficult procedure. But there are options. First, if you don't yet have a tattoo, you should consider the difficulty of removal before getting one. If you already have one that you don't want any more, you don't necessarily have to get it removed. There are alternatives, such as getting a cover-up tattoo or altering the existing one.

The removal process can also be strange. Most people getting a tattoo removed are doing so for the first time and, therefore, may be wary about undergoing a medical procedure. Postprocedure, they may worry that the side effects of their treatment are abnormal.

For these reasons, it can be a good idea to reach out to others who have gone through the same process. Talking to friends or acquaintances who have gotten tattoos removed is a good step, as is joining online tattoo removal support groups. If participating in an online group, remember that maintaining one's privacy online is important above all else. It's never a good idea to share personal information or photographs with strangers on the internet.

REMOVAL AND SCARRING

Everyone who goes to get a tattoo removed hopes for the best. Sometimes, however, tattoo removal

Tattoo removal can sometimes produce permanent markings, such as hypertrophic scars, which are raised above the surrounding skin.

can result in scars and other skin blemishes. For many people, a scar is preferable to an unwanted tattoo. Scars from tattoo removal can be divided into two categories: hypertrophic scars and keloids.

Hypertrophic scars occur when skin that is regenerating grows larger cells than normal. As a result, the scars appear to be slightly raised. In time, hypertrophic scars can fade away and even be tattooed over.

Keloid scars, however, are more severe. They are noticeably raised from the surrounding skin and are firm to the touch. They can even get worse if they are subjected to further injury, which means that they cannot be tattooed over.

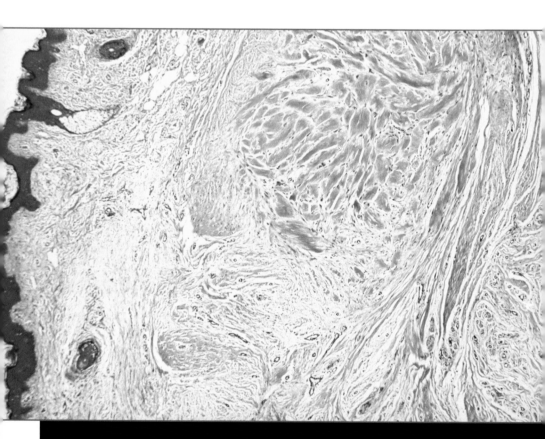

This microscopic image of a keloid scar shows the tough, fibrous protein collagen that forms in the skin.

Generally, people with dark skin are more prone to developing keloid scars as a result of tattoo removal surgery than people with fair skin. The more severe an injury, the greater the chance that scars will form as a result. The formation of scars is influenced by a number of factors, including the severity of the wound, the individual's age, and the location of the scar on his or her body.

Many people with scars want to remove them—or at least reduce the appearance of them. Unfortunately, there is only so much that can be done to accomplish this, and anyone hoping to fade or otherwise reduce the scarring should be realistic about what the results will be. Scars can be made smaller surgically, although this is often only carried out in extreme cases. Sometimes, they can be reduced with treatments such as laser therapy and dermabrasion, as well as steroid injections. As a simple measure, protecting scars with sunscreen can help make them less visible, as scars don't tan the way the surrounding skin does.

Many over-the-counter creams and ointments claim to fade scars, but the FDA hasn't reviewed a good number of them. People who are looking for products that will effectively reduce the appearance of scars should use only those that are recommended by their physician.

COVERING IT UP

Tattoo artists can often cover up unwanted or inexpertly applied tattoos with new tattoos. For people who don't mind

THE WORLD OF HENNA

Henna has been used to dye hair and skin for thousands of years. In India, Pakistan, and Bangladesh, a paste made of the plant is applied to the arms and hands of brides, creating elaborate and beautiful designs. This art is known as *mehndi*. Women have mehndi done for weddings, festivals, and other special occasions. As opposed to tattoos, henna is applied to the surface of the skin, rather than being injected directly into the dermis.

After being applied to the skin, henna is allowed to set. Then the paste can be washed off. Although it isn't permanent, henna lasts for a while—usually for about two weeks. In its natural form, henna leaves a dark brown or dark orange mark on the skin. There are some forms of henna that come in different colors, but be warned that these are artificially colored. For instance, there is a demand for black henna, but there is no way to make it naturally. So companies add a number of synthetic chemicals in order to make this kind of henna, which can cause allergic reactions in some people. For this reason, it's a good idea to test out any henna beforehand on a small patch of skin. After all, no one wants elaborate, henna-colored blisters on their arms and hands!

When applying henna, it is important to make sure that the skin is clean, as dirt and natural skin oils can keep henna from having full contact with the skin. Body hair can also interfere with its application. Many people choose to have a professional apply henna, but it is possible to apply henna to one's own skin. Usually, a design is worked out and drawn on ahead of time. Some people use hecto- graph paper, which is a paper with dye on it, to transfer a design onto their skin. It's good to work out the design before applying the henna, since the skin starts absorbing it fairly quickly and mistakes will show up. Henna needs to set in order to properly stain the skin. This takes four to twelve hours. Some people use a hair dryer to speed up the process. Others put a sealant on their skin to help the henna set. The easiest method is to spray the design with hairspray.

having a tattoo but want to get rid of the one they have, cover-ups can be a good option. Some tattoo artists excel at doing cover-up tattoos, and their work can be extremely effective. If everything goes well, the unwanted tattoo can be completely covered with a new design. Skilled artists can also "correct" poorly done tattoos.

Anyone thinking of getting a cover-up tattoo should research the prospective tattoo artists very carefully. It's best to go to an artist who has a reputation for doing effec- tive cover-up jobs. Make sure that the artist's reputation is backed up by a solid portfolio of before-and-after pho- tographs of his or her work. It is important to talk with the artist about cover-up options and make sure that one is completely happy with the design before getting the work done. After all, no one wants a bad cover-up tattoo! Imagine how annoying it would be to get a tattoo to cover a tattoo that's covering a tattoo.

Cover-up tattoos will always be larger than the designs they cover—usually significantly so. They also tend to use a lot of dark colors and black shading, which will help obscure the old, unwanted design. In addition, most cover-up tattoos need to be custom designed in order to fit the needs of the job. The tattoo being covered presents the tattoo artist with certain limitations as to what the new design can be.

Sometimes, a tattoo artist will recommend undergoing a session or two of laser removal treatments to fade the tattoo being covered up. This is especially true for tattoos that are large or have a lot of dark ink. Some tattoos, however, may not be able to be effectively covered.

The most inexpensive way to erase a tattoo is to simply cover it with clothing or makeup. Tattoos that are not on the face or hands can usually be hidden pretty easily. Some people like their tattoos but may not want to display them in certain types of social situations. For example, they might be afraid that a visible tattoo would be a liability during a job interview. Or, they might not want their great-grandmother to see the tattoo on their forearm. There is nothing inherently wrong with having a tattoo, and there's nothing wrong with wanting to cover up a tattoo on occasion.

Many people choose the placement and size of their tattoos so they can easily conceal them if they choose. The ankle is one such place.

Many people use makeup to cover up their tattoos when needed. This can be a somewhat time-consuming process, especially if one is not used to applying makeup. Concealer is a kind of makeup designed to be relatively opaque. It is used to cover blemishes and dark patches of skin. For instance, some people use concealer to cover dark circles under their eyes. Generally, concealer can be applied directly to the skin or over a layer of foundation makeup.

There are actually brands of makeup specifically designed to conceal tattoos, such as Ben Nye Tattoo Cover concealer makeup. Ben Nye is a company that specializes in makeup used by actors in theater or film. Its Tattoo Cover makeup was designed to obscure tattoos. Another brand of makeup is Sephora's Kat Von D Tattoo Concealer, named after the famous tattoo artist. While these brands are marketed specifically at people who want to conceal their ink, it's also possible to simply use regular concealer.

Covering up a tattoo with makeup takes some skill and practice to do well. The first step is finding a concealer that matches one's skin tone. This can be tricky, so it is best done in person at a makeup store. Don't be afraid to talk to store clerks about what shade of concealer would work the best. Ask if there are any samples available for customers to try. Covering dark tattoos can be tricky. Sometimes, the type of concealer that matches a person's skin tone won't be dark enough for his or her tattoo. Smaller tattoos are easier to cover than large ones, and tattoos that have experienced raised scarring can be tricky to conceal fully. With some practice, using concealer and foundation can be an effective way to cover up tattoos on occasion.

MAKING IT TEMPORARY

Granted, a major allure of tattoos is their permanence. The fact that they can't be easily removed is the very reason why many people want to get them in the first place. However, for those who simply want to wear ink

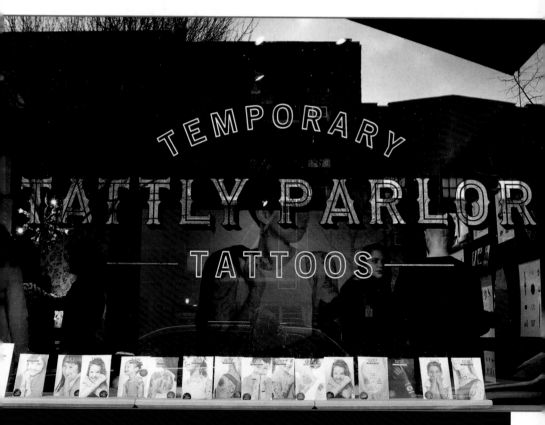

Temporary tattoos have become so popular that there are parlors, just like traditional tattoo studios, that specialize in the art.

on their skin, a temporary tattoo is a great solution. Temporary tattoos can look amazing, and the best part is that they can be removed with little more than soap and water. It isn't a commitment. A person can get temporary tattoo after temporary tattoo in the same location.

At one time, these tattoos were little more than novelty items. Today, it's possible to get temporary tattoos that range from anywhere from $10 for several generic designs to thousands of dollars for custom work by a well-known artist. Most will last for a couple of days unless efforts are taken to remove them. Temporary tattoos can also be a great way for people to test whether or not they really want a permanent tattoo. If they are comfortable with the attention they receive for having skin art, they might be good candidates for getting a permanent tattoo.

CHAPTER 2

HOW IT'S DONE

B efore getting a tattoo removed, it's important to understand how the process is done. You should know what to expect when going into the proce- dure, as well as whom to ask for professional advice.

So why are tattoos so hard to remove? After all, it's just ink, right? Why should it be so hard to erase? To understand how the process of tattoo removal works and why it is so difficult, we first need to examine how tattoos are placed into the skin.

The skin is the largest organ of the human body. It performs a number of complicated functions, from regulating body temperature to keeping moisture inside the body. The outer layer of human skin is called the epidermis. The epidermis is thin and waterproof, and it actually contains no blood vessels. The main job of the epidermis is to protect the body from getting an infection.

Since tattoo pigment is injected into the under layer of skin, the dermis, it will never wear off or fade away on its own.

When someone is getting inked, the tattoo artist isn't putting the ink into his or her epidermis. The needle of the tattoo gun penetrates the epidermis and injects the ink directly into the layer of skin below, known as the dermis.

The dermis holds the ink of a tattoo. It is full of a lot of other stuff as well—hair follicles, blood vessels, sweat glands, and more. The needle of a tattoo gun punctures the dermis thousands of times per minute, injecting enough ink into the dermis to create a design that is visible through the epidermis. Trapped inside the skin, a tattoo will last the entirety of a person's life. In fact, some Egyptian mummies have tattoos that are still recognizable after thousands of years!

AVOIDING MISTAKES

The importance of carefully choosing a tattoo—and its placement—cannot be overstated. Many people get sick of their tattoos simply because they made a foolish tattoo choice, or they got their tattoo on a part of their body, such as the neck or hands, which can't be concealed with clothing. As a result, they may find that they cannot get a job. Still other people pick a tattoo that they think will be perfect, save up their money for, and couldn't be more excited about walking into the tattoo parlor to get it. But when the tattoo gun stops buzzing and the tattoo artist swabs off the skin a final time and gives them a mirror to take a look at their new tattoo, these people don't see the design that they wanted. Instead, they see a botched piece of art—much different from the tattoo design they created (or picked off the wall of the shop). Lines that should be straight are wavy, parts of the shading look like giant bleeding wounds, and it just looks horrible overall.

Some tattoo artists are more skilled at their art than others. With tattooing, like any other trade, the more practice an artist gets, the better he or she becomes. In this case, practice involves permanently inking tattoos into people's skin! An inexperienced or careless tattoo artist might screw up the design of a tattoo, or place a tattoo too deep. Tattoos placed too deep into the dermis are extremely painful and can look faded after they heal. In addition, the design can be slightly raised on the skin. And even if the tattoo is completely removed, it is very possible that a scar will remain.

Loni Tate was hospitalized for an infection that resulted from a tattoo she received in 2014, which left permanent scarring. She ultimately sued the tattoo parlor.

To avoid a botched tattoo, it is important to choose a good tattoo shop to go to. The two basic requirements for any tattoo shop worth going to is that it is sanitary and employs skilled artists. This might sound obvious, but many people are so focused on getting inked that they don't consider all of the things that could go wrong. Regretting a tattoo is one thing, but getting a botched tattoo is another. No one wants the design that he or she was looking forward to cherishing for the rest of his or her life ruined by a tattoo artist with poor technique.

DO YOUR RESEARCH

Today, it is easier than ever to get information on businesses. Websites such as Yelp allow anyone to review a place of business, from restaurants to bike shops to tattoo parlors. Although online reviewers are generally not experts in their field, reading a lot of reviews can give someone who desires a tattoo a general idea of what he or she can expect when choosing a tattoo shop.

After locating a shop that looks promising, make sure to visit beforehand and get an idea of the cleanliness of the shop. A dirty shop (or a shop with unhygienic tattoo artists) is definitely not a good place to get a tattoo. When a tattoo is first applied, it is essentially a wound on the body, and it should be treated as such. No one would consent to being operated on by a grubby surgeon in a filthy, smoky hospital. And no one should consent to getting a tattoo in a shop that isn't a sterile environment. If the tattoo area becomes infected, it can result in faded-looking ink, scarring, and other complications.

The ink used by professional tattoo parlors is much safer than that used by amateur tattoo artists, who often simply use India ink—or, even worse, break open a ballpoint pen. Still, even the high-quality tattoo ink used by professionals has not been approved by the U.S. Food and Drug Administration (FDA). Some people have allergic reactions to tattoo ink. According to the *New York Times*, some European researchers believe that when tattoo ink is broken up by lasers, it can sometimes create dangerous, sometimes carcinogenic, or cancer-causing, byproducts that are absorbed by the body. It is a good idea to talk to a doctor about the possible harmful side effects of getting a tattoo—or getting a tattoo removed.

When planning a design, be sure to pick something that can be executed properly. Perfectly round circles are difficult for tattoo artists to pull off. In fact, for Japanese calligraphers, the ability to draw a perfect circle marks them as masters of their craft, and calligraphic masters are few and far between. Perfect parallel lines and grids are also extremely difficult for tattoo artists to execute properly.

Finally, it is important to review the tattoo artist's portfolio. A portfolio is a collection of photographs documenting a tattoo artist's work. Tattoo shops should have each artist's portfolio available for customers to peruse. If his or her work looks less than stellar, it is best to find a more competent tattoo artist.

A tattoo artist first applies the tattoo design to the customer's skin with a stencil. Then the artist should show the design to the customer before applying it to his or her skin. This is the customer's last chance to look over the design and make sure that he or she still likes

To avoid getting a botched tattoo or risking your health, visit the tattoo shop beforehand. It should be professionally run, well reviewed, and clean.

it. It is also the customer's last chance to catch any mistakes or spelling errors—nothing is more embarrassing than a misspelled tattoo!

DECIDING TO GET IT REMOVED

There is no sure way to know how one will feel about a tattoo a few years after getting it. A design that seemed like it would make an awesome tattoo sometimes just doesn't look very good when it is inked into one's skin. Also, people's tastes change over time.

Tattoos are permanent but your tastes are not. Consider how you might feel about your decision to get one well into the future.

The stuff that seemed cool when they were younger might not seem so cool as they get older. Just think about it: most seventeen-year-olds like music that is different from what they listened to when they were twelve. They also dress differently, do different things for fun, and have different posters on their walls—tastes can change a lot in five years. The same holds true for tattoos. Though not impossible, the chances are pretty slim that someone will, at the age of twenty-two, still be into a tattoo that he or she got at seventeen. Getting a tattoo is a big deal, and getting a tattoo removed is also a big decision. It is expensive, painful, and inconvenient.

It is difficult to say how long the removal will take. Complicated tattoos with many colors might require more than a dozen visits to remove, and even then it might be impossible to remove them completely. A simple black ink tattoo might require only a couple of visits, but the removal process might leave a visible scar.

Anyone getting a tattoo removed needs to have realistic expectations going into the process. When deciding on tattoo removal, it can be a good idea to talk to someone who has actually gotten a tattoo removed. Find out what the person's experience of tattoo removal was, if he or she has any advice, and if he or she can recommend a good doctor to perform the removal. It can also be helpful to look online for information about tattoo removal. Remember that it can be difficult to verify information found on the internet, and decisions shouldn't be based solely on online reviews, especially not for something as serious as tattoo removal. Before deciding on anything, it is of paramount importance that anyone wanting to erase his or her ink talk to a doctor.

Some dermatologists and cosmetic surgeons are skilled at tattoo removal. After finding a doctor to perform the procedure, it is important to schedule a consultation to discuss the options. The doctor can estimate how long the removal process will take and explain what to expect when undergoing treatment. Be aware that current tattoo removal technology cannot provide a pain-free tattoo removal experience. This might be possible someday, but it is not possible right now. Any doctor worth visiting should explain what the removal process actually entails, including the unpleasant parts. Anything less would be dishonest.

TIME AND MONEY

The cost of tattoo removal depends on a number of factors. The first factor in determining the cost is the doctor—everyone has different prices for tattoo removal. Sometimes, this is based on the quality of care. It's possible that a veteran doctor using the most up-to-date equipment might be more expensive than a less experienced doctor. It is very important to talk frankly with the doctor about the cost of the removal. Tattoo removal is generally considered to be elective surgery, which is seldom covered by health insurance. If money is an issue, shop around.

The most significant factor in calculating the cost of removing a tattoo is the size and complexity of the tattoo. Large tattoos simply take longer to remove, which equals more work for the person performing the procedure. In addition, not all tattoo inks can be effectively removed by the same kind of laser. Doctors may have to use different lasers on different kinds of inks. Different colors of ink respond to different wavelengths of laser, so the removal of multicolored tattoos can be fairly complicated.

Generally, amateur tattoos are more difficult to remove than professional ones. Some amateur artists use tattoo guns, but most simply wrap a needle in some thread, dip it in ink, and apply the tattoo by stabbing the skin over and over again! This usually results in a pretty lousy tattoo. It also means that the ink is not all set in the dermis at the same depth, making it more difficult for doctors to target the ink with a laser.

Another factor in determining the cost of tattoo removal is how many visits it will take. Large or complex tattoos will probably require multiple visits. It is likely that the price quoted will be per treatment, as opposed to a flat rate for the full removal of the tattoo. Sometimes, it's possible for a doctor to be able to estimate how many treatments will be needed to laser off a tattoo. More often, though, a doctor will need to see how the tattoo responds to treatment. Still, some tattoos can be more stubborn than others. Even the kind of tattoo ink used can influence the removal process.

Despite these variables, a doctor should be able to set a price for each treatment and hopefully be able to estimate how many treatments the entire process will take. Yet there is no telling how many treatments will go into any given removal process. Tattoo removal can run into the thousands of dollars.

Tattoo removal can also be time consuming. Multiple visits are usually necessary, and typically, it's recommended that each visit is a month apart. It might take more than a year to fully remove the tattoo. Each treatment usually takes only a few minutes, although treating a large tattoo might take thirty to forty-five minutes. Many doctors will inject the area of the removal site with the painkiller lidocaine. Patients have the right to request anesthetics such as lidocaine if they want a relatively pain-free procedure. During the procedure, patients lie on a table or sit in a chair, and wear dark glasses to protect their eyes from harmful light.

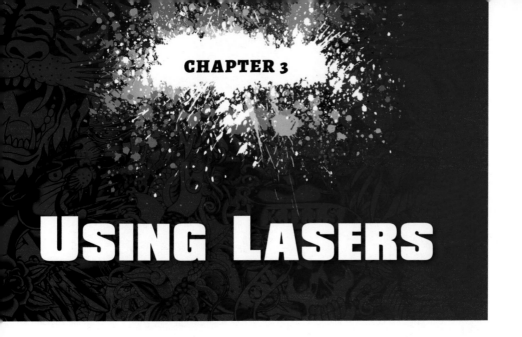

CHAPTER 3

USING LASERS

Today, using lasers to remove tattoos is the most popular method. One major reason is that it's the least invasive, meaning it doesn't puncture the skin. Lasers are used in all sorts of ways. They're used in appliances, by police officers to measure how fast cars are going, and by doctors to perform surgery.

The precise nature of lasers makes them ideal for surgical use. Today, surgeons around the world use lasers. Surgical lasers can cut and cauterize flesh, as well as penetrate the skin without making an incision. Surgeries that used to be extremely invasive and require a great deal of recovery time have been greatly simplified, thanks to lasers. For instance, the surgical removal of cataracts from the eye used to be very painful and required that the patient keep his or her eyes bandaged for days. Today, cataract removal is generally an outpatient surgery, meaning the patient gets to go

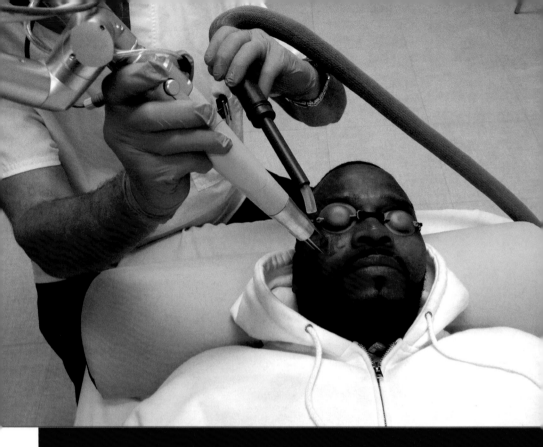

Carefully consider your tattoo placement. Though laser tattoo removal is noninvasive, it can be painful and leave scars.

home the same day. It is expected that laser technology will continue to advance, becoming even more sophisticated than it is now.

Some lasers are more specialized than others. For instance, a laser used in a simple laser pointer is very low intensity, as its function is merely to project a dot onto a nearby surface. A laser used for optical surgery, on the other hand, is designed for precision use.

The lasers used for tattoo removal work by breaking up the tattoo ink stored in the dermis. After the ink

FINDING THE RIGHT PROFESSIONAL

Just as it is important to find a good tattoo artist when getting a tattoo, it is important to shop around and find a good place to remove it. An often overlooked source of information might be a local tattoo parlor—few people know more about tattooing than the tattoo artists themselves. They may be able to recommend a trustworthy place to get a tattoo removed. In fact, some tattoo artists may have had tattoos removed themselves! Actual referrals from others who have gotten tattoos removed might be the best way to find a place.

Before getting a tattoo removed, speak to a professional, such as a dermatologist, about the risks and the best method of treatment.

Finding a place that performs laser tattoo removal is only the first step, however. Once a likely place has been located, it's good to talk to the person who will be doing the procedure.

Ask the person lots of questions, and be sure to find out how experienced he or she is. If he or she is new on the job, it might be better to go somewhere else. Doctors should be willing to answer any questions they are asked, both about the procedure and the equipment they use.

Tattoo removal technology has evolved greatly from the days when the only option was to have the tattoo actually cut out of the skin. As time goes on, tattoo removal technology only grows more and more sophisticated. Ask what kind of equipment is used in the office and research it online—is it currently the most advanced on the market? Or is it obsolete? It's best to go to a place that has the most cutting-edge equipment available.

molecules are broken up, they are reabsorbed by the body. This causes the tattoo to fade—in some cases, it eventually can be removed completely. A skilled doctor can make sure that the laser targets only the areas of the skin where the tattoo ink is stored.

The ability for lasers to be wielded in a controlled manner makes laser tattoo removal a process with many benefits and few drawbacks. It is generally effective and safe. There is no bleeding, and with the proper care, there is almost no risk of complications following the procedure. Best of all, out of all the varieties of tattoo removal currently available, laser removal leaves the least amount of scarring afterward.

Q-SWITCHED LASERS

Most clinics use Q-switched lasers to remove tattoos. These types of lasers produce intense pulses of energy for very brief periods of time, sometimes for only nanoseconds. Different kinds of Q-switched lasers are effective on different kinds of tattoo pigments. (They can also be used to target other skin pigments, such as age spots.)

Q-switched ruby lasers and Q-switched alexandrite lasers are often used on darker tattoo pigments, such as black, blue, and green inks. These lasers also can remove melanin, or naturally occurring skin pigments. To lessen this effect, some physicians use Q-switched Nd:YAG lasers (the name of this laser is an acronym for "neodymium-doped yttrium aluminum garnet"). These lasers tend to be effective on red, orange, and yellow inks as well. Black ink absorbs nearly all kinds of light, so it is the easiest color to remove. Colors such as yellow and green, however, can be trickier to remove. Lasers that are gentler on the skin's natural pigment may leave less of a mark but require more treatments in order to remove the tattoo.

Some of the newest tattoo removal technologies allow doctors to switch between different kinds of lasers

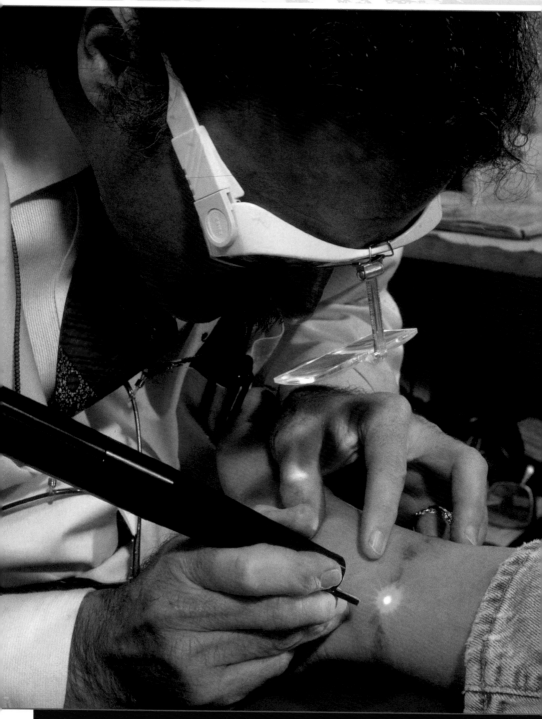

Q-switched lasers are an increasingly popular method of tattoo removal. Though this method may require more visits, it often leaves less scarring than other procedures.

with a single machine, called the VersaPulse C. The VersaPulse C is generally effective in removing different colors of tattoo ink, and it has a cooling system that minimizes damage to the epidermis, resulting in less skin damage from the treatment.

PROPER SKIN CARE

After each session, it is important to take proper care of the affected skin. Immediately following treatment, the skin may be red, swollen, and sore—some people experience bruising. (A cold compress, such as an ice pack, can relieve some of this discomfort.) It's not uncommon to discover that scabs or blisters have formed over the affected area. Also, the area that has been treated might appear to be lightened. Usually, this is only temporary.

Much like it's best to treat new tattoos like injuries until they are properly healed, it's important to take good care of tattoos undergoing the process of laser removal. This can help prevent infection and lessen the chance of complications. Talk to a physician to see what kinds of bandages, dressings, and medications should be purchased in order to care for the affected area. Doctors will often recommend gauze and medical tape to cover the tattoo, and topical antibiotics.

Depending on the size and location of the tattoo being removed, there is a chance that certain activi-

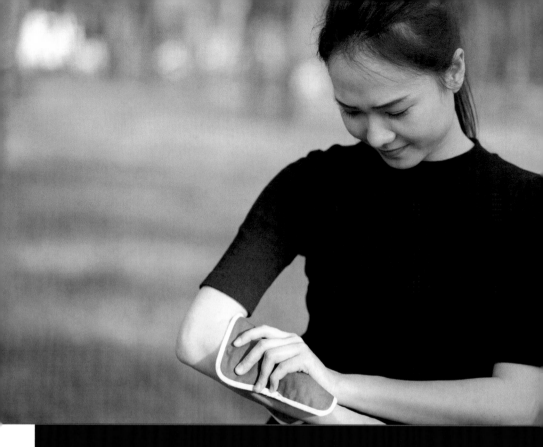

Swelling and soreness are common results of getting a tattoo. Using a cold compress can often ease the discomfort.

ties will need to be avoided until the healing process is complete. For instance, if the tattoo is located on a person's chest, he or she might want to sleep on his or her back for a few days until the skin has healed. Many of the activities that should be avoided are the same as those that would be foregone after first getting a tattoo. So no swimming for a while, avoid direct sunlight, do not take aspirin (which can worsen bleeding or bruising), and do not apply any medications to the affected area that are not first recommended or approved by the physician. Also, avoid irritating the affected area by picking at it or scratching it. Although the area will probably heal in about six to eight weeks, it's a good idea to cover it for three months with sunblock that has an SPF rating of no less than 25. This can help prevent the affected area from getting sun damaged, while allowing the skin to breathe, free of a bandage.

WHAT ARE THE SIDE EFFECTS?

Because laser removal is totally noninvasive, many people optimistically hope that their skin will look exactly the way that it did before they got the tattoo. Sadly, this is seldom the case. While it is often possible to completely remove tattoos, it is rare that they can be removed without leaving some sort of mark. After the postremoval scabs and blisters heal completely, it's possible to take a look at how the skin will appear in the long run. Sometimes, laser removal procedures cause scarring, or they permanently lighten the skin. Other times, the procedures can actually change the texture of the skin. Of course, everyone who wants his or her tattoos removed hopes for the best—that the skin will look exactly the way it did … almost as if he or she had never gotten a tattoo. Remember, the decision to get a tattoo is not one

Though tattoos can be removed, they are still permanent in a sen
is because removal doesn't completely eliminate the tattoo, as sh
this before-and-after photo.

to be taken lightly. Once that tattoo is inked, your skin will never be the same again.

Some people choose to use laser removal to progressively lighten their tattoos until they can be covered up with other tattoos. Others find that their tattoos simply do not respond to laser removal, so they need to opt for a different kind of procedure, which can include dermabrasion and excision. Others decide to try their luck with newer treatment procedures, such as intense pulsed light therapy.

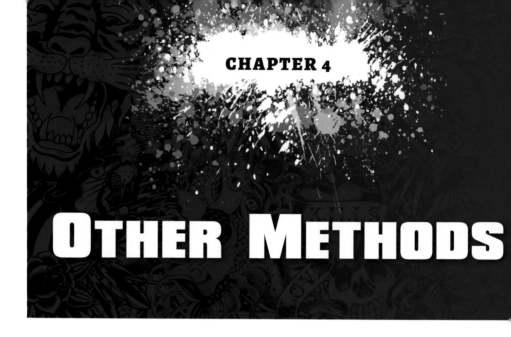

CHAPTER 4

OTHER METHODS

Though lasers are the most popular method used in tattoo removal, there are other ways to go about the process. Before choosing one of these methods though, it's important to understand what they are, and their pros and cons.

New technologies promise to revolutionize the field of tattoo removal. New laser technologies could make lasers more precise. Some companies are working on creating creams that could be applied to the surface of the skin to remove the tattoo. Many hope that the day will come when technology will permit tattoos to be removed completely, with little pain or other negative side effects. Right now, however, there are only a few proven tattoo removal methods besides laser removal. These are intense pulsed light therapy, excision, and dermabrasion.

INTENSE PULSED LIGHT THERAPY (IPL)

Intense pulsed light (IPL) therapy is used by dermatologists to remove skin blemishes, such as age spots and moles. Although sometimes confused with laser removal, IPL therapy is somewhat different. Instead of a laser, this form of therapy uses intense light to penetrate the skin. And unlike laser removal, a gel is applied over the area to be treated before it is hit with pulses of light. Proponents of IPL therapy believe that the pulses of light can be adjusted more precisely for individual patients.

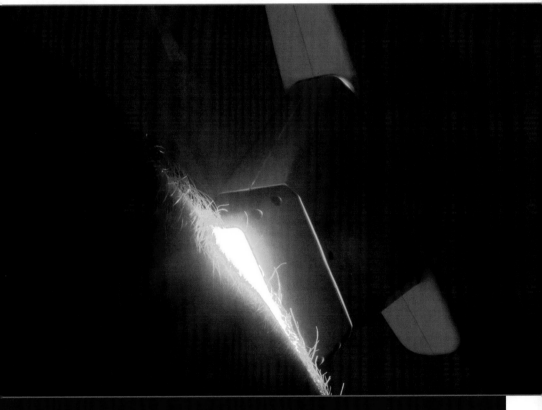

Intense pulsed light (IPL) therapy is often used to remove blemishes on the skin, such as age spots. However, it is also used as a method for tattoo removal.

Like laser removal, however, IPL therapy is painful. Some patients opt for anesthesia to lessen the pain of the light pulses. Some say that IPL therapy is more effective than laser removal, but it isn't ideal for all patients. In some cases, it can cause an uneven increase in skin pigmentation, and patients with darker skin tones usually experience complications. Usually, candidates for IPL treatment first undergo a test treatment, where a single pulse of light is applied to a patch of skin to see if there will be any unwanted pigmentation side effects. Also, people who take blood-thinning medication or who are diabetics cannot receive IPL treatment.

It is believed that IPL treatments can remove tattoos in fewer sessions than laser treatments can. Good news, right? However, there is a major drawback to IPL therapy, even for those who are eligible for it: the price. Most places charge for each pulse of light, rather than per session. This means that the size of the tattoo being removed is a major factor in how much its removal will cost. The cost of each pulse can run upward of $10. Also, many places have a minimum charge for each visit, which can be more than $100. The fact that IPL therapy is so expensive and not appropriate for all skin types has ensured that laser treatment is still the most commonly used method of tattoo removal. Some people think that IPL therapy may someday become more popular than laser removal for getting rid of unwanted ink. Should this

BEWARE!

It is absolutely necessary to consult with qualified, experienced dermatologists and other doctors before choosing a method of tattoo removal.

Tattoo removal is always expensive and is frequently painful. There is no getting around these facts. Searching for qualified doctors with the latest equipment can take time and patience, and getting the proper treatment costs money—and these costs will most likely not be reimbursed by health insurance. Some removal methods produce unsightly scabs and

(continued on the next page)

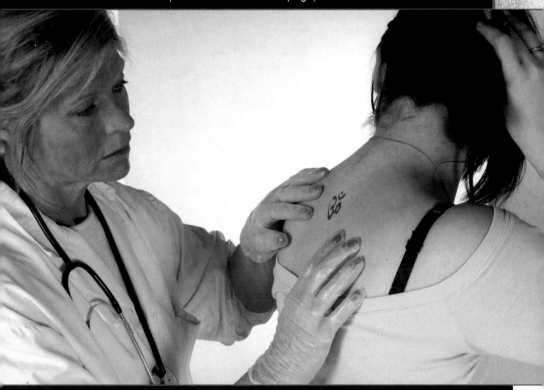

When considering tattoo removal, it's important to consult with a professional, including your physician, for the recommended course of treatment.

(continued from the previous page)

blisters, which makes some people uneasy. Simply put, getting a tattoo removed is a massive inconvenience, and many people are tempted to seek out alternative treatments that are easier and less expensive than proven tattoo removal methods.

There are a number of products out there—many of which are being sold only on the internet—that claim to remove tattoos cheaply, quickly, and painlessly. The overwhelming majority of these products has not undergone proper tests and has not been approved by the FDA. They may be hazardous to one's health, and little evidence exists to prove that they actually work. After all, if they worked the way they promised, surely they would be just as popular as laser removal.

Some of the most common products that promise to erase unwanted ink are tattoo removal creams. Most of these products claim that they can fade tattoos by simply being applied topically on the skin. Unless a doctor recommends these creams, they should be regarded with suspicion at the very least and probably be avoided altogether.

happen, it's likely that the cost of IPL treatments will drop. Until then, however, it remains one of the most expensive, albeit effective, means of tattoo removal.

Perhaps someday, IPL therapy will be fine-tuned to the extent that everyone can benefit from it. In the meantime, it is definitely an option for people with very fair skin. It is rare that IPL therapy results in scabs or bleeding, although sometimes the skin of the affected area undergoes pigmentation changes, becoming lighter or darker.

EXCISION, OR REMOVING THE SKIN

Prior to the invention of noninvasive forms of tattoo removal, there was no "easy" way to get rid of a tattoo. Since doctors could not target the tattoo ink in the skin, their only recourse was to simply remove the skin where the tattoo was. Although rarely used today, surgical excision can be effective in removing tattoos that won't respond to any other form of treatment.

Unlike laser removal and IPL therapy, excision is extremely invasive and must be performed by a surgeon. The doctor performing the surgery uses a scalpel to cut the tattoo out of the patient's skin and then closes the wound. Sometimes, an inflatable sac is inserted under the skin and blown up, stretching the skin of the tattoo in order to allow surgeons to remove it with greater precision. Because of how invasive this procedure is, few people opt for it as their first choice. Excision always leaves a scar, although some people are more prone to scarring than others. The scar left by excision depends largely on the size of the tattoo and its location on the body.

Excision works better on small tattoos than large ones. Because it is cheaper than laser removal, some people with smaller tattoos simply elect to get them excised. Sure, it may leave a scar, but it only takes a single visit and it's easier on the wallet. However, like other forms of tattoo removal, excision is considered elective surgery and, therefore, is not covered by most health insurance. As such, it is important to have a frank talk with the doctor about the costs of the procedure and to make sure that he or she can competently perform the procedure.

THE DERMABRASION PROCESS

Another extremely invasive tattoo removal procedure is known as dermabrasion. This procedure involves the use of a spinning disk that basically "sands" the skin off of the body. Generally, dermabrasion is not the first procedure recommended for tattoo removal. Unlike excision, dermabrasion usually requires several sessions to yield results. And while it takes only seven to ten days for the scabbed-over skin to heal, it will remain visibly red or pink for two to three months. Beyond that, it can take up to six months to truly be able to gauge the final result of the treatments. This treatment was not originally designed with tattoo removal in mind. Instead, it was to help correct skin damaged by acne scars or other blemishes, as the skin generally grows back smoother after this proce-dure.

It is unlikely that a doctor would recommend derm-abrasion to remove a tattoo, but it is possible. Some see dermabrasion as a sort of compromise between laser removal and excision. It's definitely important to go to an experienced surgeon, ask a lot of questions, and ensure that the doctor takes a thorough medical history.

For many people, the initially cosmetically hideous results of dermabrasion are a major downside of the procedure. However, after the scab has healed, there are steps that can be taken to make the skin appear more even-toned until the healing process is complete. For instance, some people use hypoallergenic makeup to even out the skin tone in the affected area. During the healing process, it is important to keep the affected area out of the sun, or cover it with a sunblock that has an SPF of at least 25.

FADING THE TATTOO

Saline injections can help lighten existing tattoos. Saline is a completely sterile solution of sodium chloride in water. In a very simple procedure, the saline is injected into an existing tattoo. Sometimes, this can work to break up the tattoo, effectively making it fade. The benefits of getting saline injections are that they involve almost no risk if performed properly, are much less painful than other methods, and are minimally invasive. In addition, the recovery time is more or less equal to the recovery time of getting a tattoo.

Getting saline injections is generally cheaper than other tattoo removal methods. However, this procedure cannot fully remove a tattoo. Instead, it can effectively

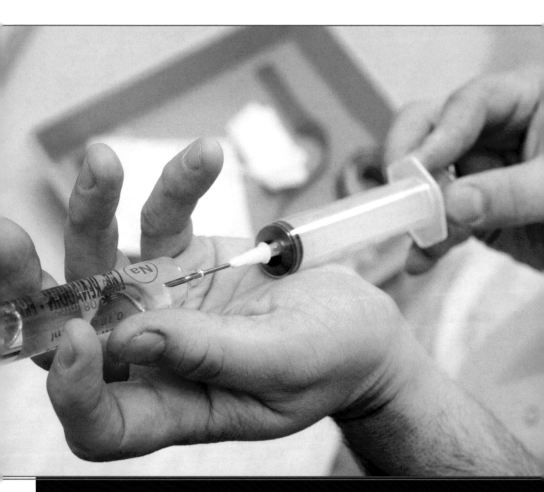

A less intensive method of tattoo removal is having saline injections, which fade the tattoo over time.

"blur" the old tattoo, making it easier for a cover-up tattoo to be applied. There is little chance that saline injections will result in changes of the skin's texture and pigmentation, or result in any scarring. The results can be a bit unpredictable, but many people who opt for saline injections are of the opinion that there is little to lose by trying them out.

Since tattoo removal is so painful, expensive, and time-consuming, what can be done to avoid it? There are two ways: The first is to not get any tattoos, and the second is to get a tattoo that won't cause regrets later on. Tattoo choices should be thought out very carefully. One simple way to prevent tattoo regret is to pick a design, get a copy of it, and hang it on the wall. If the design still seems appealing after six months, maybe it's OK to go ahead and start looking for a good tattoo artist to ink it. The design should still seem cool in a year, ten years, and even fifty years.

GLOSSARY

ANESTHETIC A substance that provides relief from, or insensitivity to, pain.

CARCINOGENIC Cancer-causing.

CATARACT A clouding of the eye's lens that often comes with age.

CAUTERIZE To seal skin by burning it.

DERMABRASION The removal of skin with a spinning abrasive disc. Dermabrasion is meant to remove damaged skin so that new skin can grow back and replace it.

DERMIS The layer of skin protected by the epidermis, which holds the ink of a tattoo.

EPIDERMIS The outermost layer of skin.

EXCISION A surgical procedure that involves cutting out the skin that holds the tattoo and closing up the wound.

HENNA A plant-based dye used to color skin and hair.

INCISION In surgery, a cut made into the body.

INDIA INK A simple black ink, made from black soot, that was traditionally used for drawing.

INVASIVE Describing any kind of medical procedure that involves cutting into or inserting anything into the human body.

LASER A generated beam of electromagnetic radiation.

MAINSTREAM Belonging to the culture shared by the majority of people.

PIGMENT The matter in a cell or tissue that gives color in human skin.

PROCEDURE A specific medical operation.

SCALPEL A tool used by surgeons to make incisions.

SCAR A mark on the skin resulting from tissue regenerating after an injury. Scars stand out from the skin that surrounds them.

STERILE Free of contaminates.

WOUND An injury that inflicts a cut or tear in the skin.

FOR MORE INFORMATION

Alliance of Professional Tattooists
22052 W. 66th Street, Suite 225
Shawnee, KS 66226
(816) 979-1300
Website: http://www.safe-tattoos.com
The Alliance of Professional Tattooists is dedicated to
providing information to artists and the public at large
about tattooing.

American Academy of Dermatology
930 East Woodfield Road
PO Box 4014
Schaumburg, IL 60168-4014
(866) 503-7546
Website: http://www.aad.org
The academy's website features a directory of derma-
tologists and advice on getting tattoos on its website.

Canadian Public Health Association
404-1525 Carling Ave.
Ottawa, ON K1Z 8R9
Canada
(613) 725-3769
Website: http://www.cpha.ca/en/default.aspx
This nongovernmental public health association pub-
lishes information about tattoo safety guidelines at http:
//www.cpha.ca/en/portals/hiv/prevention/faq08.aspx.

Centers for Disease Control and Prevention (CDC)
1600 Clifton Road
Atlanta, GA 30329-4027
(800) 232-4636
Website: http://www.cdc.gov
The CDC monitors public health issues and works to
educate the public, enhance public safety, and pro-
mote healthy behavior. It is a source of information
about any side effects resulting from tattoo removal.

National Tattoo Association
485 Business Park Lane
Allentown, PA 18109-9120
(610) 433-7261
Website: http://nationaltattooassociation.com
The association provides tattoo safety information,
news, contact information for professionals, and pic-
tures of the work of member tattooists in the United
States, Canada, and other countries.

Public Health Agency of Canada
130 Colonnade Road
A.L. 6501H
Ottawa, Ontario K1A 0K9
(844) 280-5020
Website: https://www.canada.ca/en/public-health.html
The agency's website includes reports on tattooing,

blood-borne diseases including hepatitis and HIV,
and other information.

Society of Permanent Cosmetic Professionals
69 N. Broadway St.
Des Plaines, IL 60016
(847) 635-1330
Website: http://www.spcp.org
The society provides information about cosmetic tattooing
and a directory of professionals. The society also has a
Canadian directory of tattoo professionals.

Tattoo Archive
618 West 4th Street
Winston-Salem, NC 27101
(336) 722-4422
Website: http://www.tattooarchive.com/contact_us.htm
The Tattoo Archive works to preserve tattoo history.

FOR FURTHER READING

Abdoyan, Brenda. *Teach Yourself Henna Tattoo: Making Mehndi Art with Easy-to-Follow Instructions, Patterns, and Projects*. East Petersburg, PA: Design Originals, 2016.

Angell, Tom, and Patrick Dalton. *London Tattoo Guide*. London, England: Hardie Grant Books, 2017.

Foster, Victoria. *Tatouage—Blossom 102 Temporary Tattoos of Flowers and Plants*. London, England: Laurence King Publishing, 2017.

Friedman, Anna F. *The World Atlas of Tattoo*. New Haven, CT: Yale University Press, 2015.

Gilbert, Steve. *The Tattoo History Source Book*. New York, NY: Powerhouse Books, 2004.

Green, Terisa. Ink: *The Not-Just-Skin-Deep Guide to Getting a Tattoo*. New York, NY: NAL Trade, 2006.

Hardy, Don Ed. *Ed Hardy Art for Life*. Kempen, Germany: teNeues, 2009.

Hardy, Lal. *The Mammoth Book of Tattoos*. Philadelphia, PA: Running Press, 2009.

Sawyer, Sarah. *Frequently Asked Questions About Body Piercing and Tattooing*. New York, NY: Rosen Publishing, 2009.

Shaw, Jonathan. *Vintage Tattoo Flash: 100 Years of Traditional Tattoos from the Collection of Jonathan Shaw*. Brooklyn, NY: PowerHouse Books, 2016.

Smith, Trent, and Ashley Tyson. *The Tattoo Dictionary: An A-Z Guide to Choosing Your Tattoo*. New York, NY: Hachette Book Group, 2016.

Superior Tattoo. *Tattoo Bible: Book One*. Stillwater, MN: Wolfgang Publications, 2009.

Von D, Kat. *Go Big or Go Home: Taking Risks in Life, Love, and Tattooing*. New York, NY: Harper Design, 2013.

Yi, Jian. *One Million Tattoos*. New York, NY: Thunder Bay Press, 2010.

BIBLIOGRAPHY

Finn, Ericka. *The Complete Guide to Tattoo Removal*. Pasadena, CA: Zibi Books, 2007.

Grant, Tim. "Tattoos, Piercings Bad Sign for Job: Though Acceptance Is Growing, Many Firms Still Are Not Tolerant." *Detroit News*, August 19, 2010. http://www.detnews.com.

Hudson, Karen L. *Living Canvas: Your Total Guide to Tattoos, Piercings, and Body Modification*. Berkeley, CA: Seal Press, 2009.

Kat von D Makeup Collection. Retrieved December 8, 2017. https://www.katvondbeauty.com.

La Ferla, Ruth. "Tattooed for a Day, Wild for a Night." *New York Times*, January 24, 2008. http://www.nytimes.com/2008/01/24/fashion/24TATTOO.html.

Lineberry, Cate. "Tattoos: The Ancient and Mysterious History." Smithsonian.com, January 1, 2007. http://www.smithsonianmag.com/history-archaeology/tattoo.html.

Mayo Clinic. "Cosmetic Surgery: Dermabrasion at Mayo Clinic." Retrieved July 1, 2010. http://www.mayoclinic.org/cosmetic-surgery/dermabrasion.html.

Nocera, Kate. "Teen Kimberly Vlaminck with 56 Star Tattoos on Her Face Admits She Wanted Them the Whole Time." *New York Daily News*, June 23, 2009. http://www.nydailynews.com.

Padilla, Darcy. "Erasing Gang Tattoos from Faces and Hands." *New York Times*, May 8, 1994. http://www.nytimes.com/1994/05/08/us/erasing-gang-tattoos-from-faces-and-hands.html.

Reardon, John. *Getting a Tattoo: The Complete Idiot's Guide*. New York, NY: Penguin, 2008.

Singer, Natasha. "Erasing Tattoos, Out of Regret or for a New Canvas." *New York Times*, June 17, 2007. http://www.nytimes.com.

Statistics Brain. August 13, 2016. https://www.statisticbrain.com/tattoo-statistics.

U.S. Food and Drug Administration. "Tattoos & Permanent Makeup." June 23, 2008. http://www.fda.gov/Cosmetics/ProductandIngredientSafety/ProductInformation/ucm108530.htm.

INDEX

hypertrophic scars, 9–10

I

inks, types of, 23–24
intense pulsed light therapy (IPL), 43–47
internet, precautions with, 9, 27

K

keloids (scars), 9–10

L

laser removal
  advantages of, 34–35
  cataract removal (example), 31–32
  colors of ink and wavelengths of laser, 29
  potential dangers of, 24
  to fade a tattoo, 14, 49–51
  Q-switched lasers, 35, 37
  saline injections, 49–51

M

makeup
  to cover a tattoo, 14, 16–17
  hypoallergenic, during healing process, 49

mehndi (henna art), 12–13
methods of tattoo removal
  advantages of laser removal, 34–35
  colors of ink and wavelengths of laser, 29
  dermabrasion, 48–49
  excision, 47–48
  fading a tattoo, 14, 49–51
  intense pulsed light therapy, 43–47
  laser, 31–41
  least invasive, 31
  potential dangers of, 24
  Q-switched lasers, 35–37
  saline injections, 49–51
  Versa-Pulse C, 35, 37
mistakes, avoiding, 21–22

O

online support groups, 9

P

pain
  anesthesia for, 30
  as factor in removal, 28

parlors, tattoo, research-
ing, 23–25
pigmentation changes,
with removal, 47
precautions about choos-
ing method, 45–46

Q

Q-switched lasers, 35, 37
quality of tattoo, 7

R

referrals for profession-
als, 33
regrets for choosing to
tattoo, 4
research
cover-up tattoo artist,
13–14
parlors and artists,
23–25, 33
reviews, online, 23, 27

S

saline injections, 49–51
scarring
factors affecting, 11
Q-switched laser
removal, 36

types of, 9–11
Sephora's Kat Von D Tattoo
Concealer, 16
side effects of removal,
24, 39, 41
skin
anatomy of, 19–20
care of, after treat-
ments, 37
steroid injections to
reduce scars, 11
sunblock, 39
support groups, online, 9
surgical excision tech-
nique, 47–48

T

tanning, and scars, 11
temporary tattoos, 17–18
time as factor in removal,
28–30
treatments, number of, 29

V

Versa-Pulse C, 35, 37

ABOUT THE AUTHORS

Nicholas Faulkner is a writer living in New Jersey.

Frank Spalding is a writer from upstate New York. He has long been fascinated by the history of tattooing. When he was ten years old, he got his first temporary tattoo, the Egyptian god Set, which he applied to his forehead. He's very glad that it wasn't permanent.

PHOTO CREDITS

Cover, p. 1 Rick Loomis/Los Angeles Times/Getty Images; p. 5 Boston Globe/Getty Images; p. 9 Dr. Harout Tanielian /Science Source; p. 10 Biophoto Associates/Science Source /Getty Images; p. 15 Jon Kopaloff/FilmMagic/Getty Images; p. 17 Spencer Platt/Getty Images; p. 20 craftvision/E+/Getty Images; p. 22 ZUMA Press Inc./Alamy Stock Photo; p. 25 Pavel L Photo and Video/Shutterstock.com; p. 26 Tetra Images /Getty Images; p. 32 © AP Images; p. 33 Dmytro Zinkevych /Shutterstock.com; p. 36 Russell Curtis/Science Source; p. 38 Chutima Chaochaiya/Shutterstock.com; p. 40 Axel Koester/The New York Times/Redux; p. 43 Fanthomme Hubert/Paris Match Archive/Getty Images; p. 45 BSIP SA/Alamy Stock Photo; p. 50 BSIP/Universal Images Group; cover and interior pages Liubomyr Feshchyn/Hemera/Thinkstock (splatters), Gollfx /Shutterstock.com (tattoo design).

Design: Brian Garvey; Layout: Ellina Litmanovich; Photo Researcher: Karen Huang